# MR.MEOW'S PAWSITIVE LESSONS

## Lesson 1 - Be Yourself

Written by
Felix Checinski

Mr. Meow is a professor and a cat.

He taught many kittens whether their tails were slim or fat.

SLIM OR FAT

"Purr, my kittens, grow wise and true,
I'm here to teach wonderful things to you."

From his window perch,
on a sunny day,

he saw Konner and Kailey
laugh, leap, and play.

When he overheard them talk, he fell off his chair in shock.

"Ruff, I'm a dog, and ribbit, you're pretending to be a frog." Kailey said.

Konnor argued, "But I don't have to pretend, I can be a frog til the end!"

Konnor wondered if he could shave off his fur.
He thought about losing his soft, soothing, purr.

Konnor thought about turning his skin into
scales so green.

And Konnor thought about eating flies, an
unusual cuisine!

Konnor shouted, "Froggy is my name."
Then the kitten pair went on playing their game.

"I'll be a frog forever,"
Konnor said with a hop.
"I can do this all day and
never ever stop!"

As Mr.Meow listened, his brow wrinkled in doubt.

Outside he rushed, with a worried cat's pout.

"Who's spinning these stories, my playful pair?"

Konnor and Kailey blinked with a curious stare.

"We can be anything we want, you see."
Konnor said, his voice full of glee.

Mr.Meow shook his head. "A cat's
always a cat, there is no doubt.
Being yourself is what life's all
about."

Mr. Meow dressed up as a dog. It was almost as funny as a 5 legged frog!

"Do you like my outfit?" Mr. Meow asked. The kittens nodded and laughed, they were having a blast.

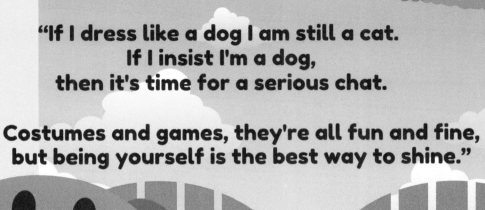

"If I dress like a dog I am still a cat.
If I insist I'm a dog,
then it's time for a serious chat.

Costumes and games, they're all fun and fine,
but being yourself is the best way to shine."

"You're right," said the kittens.
"Costumes can only change your looks."

Mr. Meow decided to show them a
couple of books.

"Cats are known for their grace and agility.

With paws that can climb and bring tranquility."

"They're masters of stealth, with eyes sharp and keen.

Their sleek fur glistens, a sight to be seen."

"Dogs, on the other hand, are loyal and true. Their barks resound with joy and protect you.

With wagging tails and a playful heart. They're a friend by your side, never to depart."

"My dear kittens don't fret and ponder, you're a cat through and through, and that's no wonder."

"Embrace your whiskers, your purrs, and your grace.

For that's what makes you part of the feline race."

With that said, the lesson came to an end,
they now know changing their identity
is only pretend.

Mr.Meow had a big smile, he knew his
lesson was important and worthwhile.

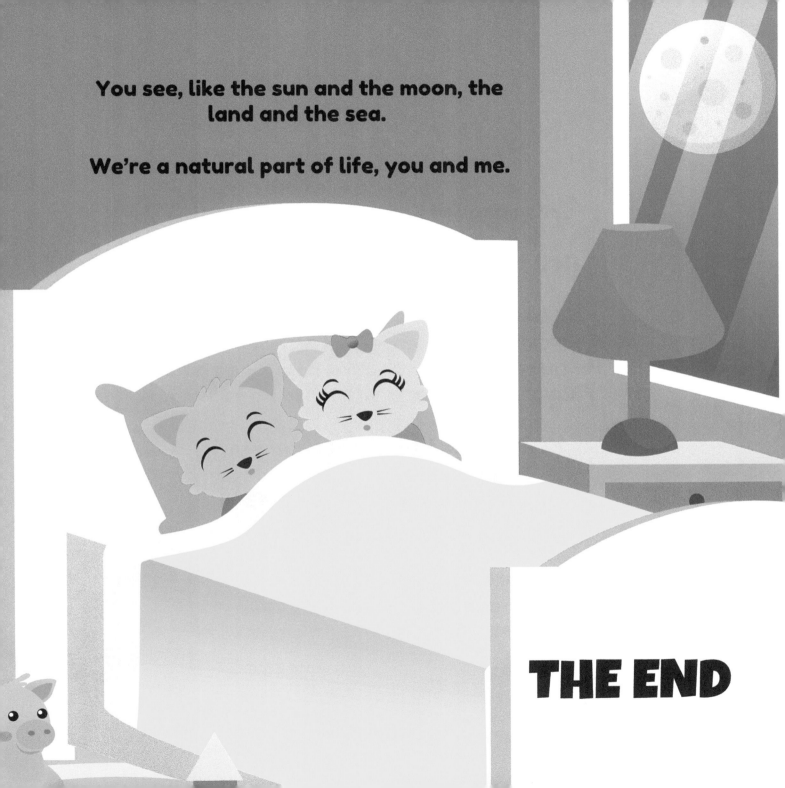

You see, like the sun and the moon, the land and the sea.

We're a natural part of life, you and me.

**THE END**

Meet Mr. Meow, a wise old cat,
Spreading love and joy, just like that!
In a topsy-turvy world we see,
He'll teach kids values and how-to-be!

No confusion here, just a family's care,
With Pawsitive Lessons, you'll be happy to share.
He's a wise professor, on a mission so bold,
Filling young hearts with wisdom to hold.

In rhymes and tales, he'll show the way,
To brighten every child's day.
So come along, let's join the fun,
Together, we'll learn, one by one.

Embrace this story, keep it near,
These lessons are valuable,
and ones all should hear!